COSMIC CANNABIS CULTIVATION

Cosmic Cannabis Cultivation

Matthew Petchinsky

Apophis Enterprises LLC

1

Cosmic Cannabis Cultivation
By: Matthew Petchinsky

Introduction: Sowing Seeds in the Cosmic Garden

Welcome to a transformative journey through the realms of horticulture and astrology, where the cultivation of cannabis meets the ancient wisdom of the cosmos. "Cosmic Cannabis Cultivation" is not merely a guide to growing cannabis—it is a philosophical exploration of how cosmic forces can synergize with agricultural practices to enhance not only the growth and potency of your plants but also your connection to the natural world. This book introduces an innovative and spiritually enriching approach to cultivating cannabis by harmonizing with the celestial influences of the moon, planets, and beyond.

The Philosophy of Cosmic Cannabis Cultivation

At the heart of this book lies the philosophy of Cosmic Cannabis Cultivation, a concept that transcends traditional planting techniques. This approach invites you to view the cannabis plant as a conduit between earthly and cosmic energies, capable of absorbing and reflecting the forces that flow through the universe. By integrating these celestial powers with the cultivation process, you can influence the lifecycle and qualities of your cannabis, creating a product that is not only superior in quality but also imbued with the vibrational signatures of the cosmos.

We delve into how ancient civilizations revered the sky and stars, drawing upon their alignments and patterns to guide their agricultural practices. Similarly, Cosmic Cannabis Cultivation revisits these ancient traditions and adapts them to modern cannabis growing, merging scientific agronomy with astrological insights to optimize the timing of planting, tending, and harvesting based on celestial cycles.

Understanding the Celestial Influence

To fully embrace this cultivation philosophy, it's crucial to understand the celestial influences that play a pivotal role in the growth of plants. This section of the book provides an overview of how celestial bodies—especially the moon and planets—exert a profound impact on plant development. From the gravitational pull that affects water absorption and nutrient uptake to the more subtle energies that influence plant bioenergetics, each aspect of celestial interaction is explored to enhance your understanding and practical application.

The lunar cycle, for instance, affects the moisture in the soil, making certain phases more suitable for seeding, while others are optimal for harvesting. Planetary alignments can also affect plant growth, with each planet offering a unique set of energies that influence various aspects of plant development and health. By aligning your cultivation practices with these celestial events, you can tap into a powerful resource that traditional methods overlook.

Navigating This Book

"Cosmic Cannabis Cultivation" is designed to be accessible and informative for readers of all backgrounds, whether you are a novice to astrology and gardening or an experienced practitioner in either field. The book is structured to guide you step by step, ensuring that you understand both the theoretical underpinnings and practical applications of cosmic cultivation.

Each chapter builds upon the last, beginning with basic concepts before advancing to more complex practices. For those unfamiliar with astrology, there is a primer to bring you up to speed on the necessary celestial knowledge. Similarly, gardening tips are tailored to accommodate both beginner and veteran cultivators, ensuring everyone can grow their cosmic cannabis effectively.

Furthermore, the book includes a variety of diagrams, tables, and illustrations to help visualize concepts and techniques. Practical tips, case studies, and real-world examples are scattered throughout to provide concrete applications of the theories discussed.

As you turn the pages of this book, you will learn not only how to cultivate cannabis in harmony with the cosmos but also how to observe and interact with the natural world in a more profound and meaningful way. This guide is a compass to navigating the celestial influences that impact your garden, helping you to sow your seeds in the cosmic garden with wisdom and confidence.

Chapter 1: Cosmic Basics for Cannabis Cultivators

Welcome to the foundational concepts of Cosmic Cannabis Cultivation. This chapter is designed to introduce you to the celestial mechanics that play a crucial role in the natural world and specifically in the cultivation of cannabis. Understanding these cosmic influences will help you to harmonize your gardening efforts with the rhythms of the universe, optimizing the life cycle of your cannabis plants from seed to harvest. We will explore the lunar cycles, planetary alignments, and astrological signs, providing you with the knowledge to tap into these cosmic forces effectively.

LUNAR CYCLES AND PLANTING

The moon's influence on agricultural practices has been acknowledged and revered by various cultures across millennia. The lunar cycle, particularly its waxing and waning, exerts significant effects on plant growth through gravitational pull and light variation, which in turn affect water absorption and seed germination.

Phases of the Moon:

1. **New Moon to First Quarter (Waxing Crescent):** This phase is optimal for planting seeds. The increasing light and gravitational pull encourage strong root growth. During this period, the sap flow in plants increases, making it an excellent time to sow seeds that benefit from good root development.
2. **First Quarter to Full Moon (Waxing Gibbous):** As the moon brightens, it's conducive to leaf growth. This phase is ideal for faster germination and vigorous growth of foliage.

3. **Full Moon to Last Quarter (Waning Gibbous)**: This period is less about growth and more about consolidation. The gravitational pull is strong but the light is decreasing, which is suitable for root development. Planting perennials or biennials can be beneficial during this phase.

4. **Last Quarter to New Moon (Waning Crescent)**: The reduced light and gravitational influence make this phase ideal for pruning, transplanting, or harvesting. The sap is low in the plant, reducing the risk of pest attacks and diseases.

Each of these phases brings a unique aspect to the growth cycle of cannabis, from germination to maturity, influencing not only the physical growth but also the biochemical development of the plant.

PLANETARY ALIGNMENTS AND THEIR INFLUENCES

Beyond the moon, the planets in our solar system also contribute their energies and influences to the life on Earth, including our plants. Each planet imparts unique characteristics based on its astrological significance and position relative to Earth.

- **Sun**: Directly influences vitality and energy. Sunlight is crucial for photosynthesis, the very basis of plant life.
- **Mercury**: Associated with communication, it influences how plants respond to environmental cues and how effectively they absorb nutrients.
- **Venus**: Often linked with growth and fertility, Venus enhances the plant's flavor and aesthetic qualities.
- **Mars**: Governs assertiveness and survival traits. It can enhance the plant's natural defenses against pests and diseases.
- **Jupiter**: Associated with expansion and abundance, beneficial for overall plant growth and yield.

- **Saturn**: Linked with structure and discipline, it helps in strengthening the plants' structural properties like stem thickness and root depth.

Understanding these influences allows cultivators to align their planting and nurturing schedules with planetary movements, optimizing the vitality and potency of their cannabis plants.

ASTROLOGICAL SIGNS AND CANNABIS CULTIVATION

Astrological signs can also provide a cosmic calendar to guide cultivation practices. Each zodiac sign imparts different energies, influencing plant growth in unique ways. Here's how you can use them:

- **Fire Signs (Aries, Leo, Sagittarius)**: Best for planting and harvesting, as they bring energy and growth.
- **Earth Signs (Taurus, Virgo, Capricorn)**: Ideal for fertilizing and planting, as they stabilize and enhance growth.
- **Air Signs (Gemini, Libra, Aquarius)**: Suitable for harvesting and pruning, as they facilitate better air flow around plants.
- **Water Signs (Cancer, Scorpio, Pisces)**: Excellent for watering and planting, as they enhance moisture absorption and root growth.

By aligning your cultivation schedule with the astrological signs, you can tap into the natural energies of the cosmos to enhance each phase of your cannabis plant's life cycle.

As we progress through "Cosmic Cannabis Cultivation," you will learn to apply these concepts practically, ensuring your cultivation efforts are as efficient and fruitful as possible. This chapter lays the groundwork for a deeper understanding of how cosmic forces can be harnessed to elevate both the spiritual and material yields of your cannabis garden.

Check out my Virtual dispensary for all your hemp needs: https://shift.store/sg1fan23477/retail

Chapter 2: Preparing the Soil - Earth Signs Taurus, Virgo, Capricorn

The preparation of soil is the foundational step in any form of cultivation, but in Cosmic Cannabis Cultivation, it goes beyond mere physical preparation. This chapter delves into how the energies of the earth signs—Taurus, Virgo, and Capricorn—can be harnessed to enhance the fertility of the soil and ensure the stability and robustness of your cannabis plants. By integrating astrological insights into traditional soil preparation techniques, we can create an optimal growing environment that is energetically aligned with the forces of the cosmos.

Earth's Fertility and Cannabis: Influence of Earth Signs

Earth signs are synonymous with stability, growth, and pragmatism. In the zodiac, Taurus, Virgo, and Capricorn each bring unique qualities that influence the physical attributes of the soil, which in turn affect plant growth:

- **Taurus**: Ruled by Venus, Taurus imparts fertility and richness. Its influence enhances the soil's ability to retain water and nutrients, making it lush and productive. For cannabis cultivation, a Taurus phase is ideal for enriching the soil with organic matter such as compost and manure, which helps build a strong, nutrient-rich foundation.
- **Virgo**: Governed by Mercury, Virgo's influence is all about precision and attention to detail. This sign enhances the structure of the soil, making it ideal for facilitating proper root growth and nutrient uptake. During Virgo phases, focus on fine-tuning the soil texture and pH levels to ensure they meet the specific needs of cannabis plants.
- **Capricorn**: Under the rule of Saturn, Capricorn contributes structure and discipline. It affects the soil's ability to support the cannabis plant's structural integrity, particularly its stems and

roots. Capricorn energy is best for incorporating minerals like calcium and magnesium, which strengthen the plant's cell walls and overall stability.

Practical Applications: Tailoring Soil Mixtures and Nutrient Regimes

Building on the energetic properties provided by the earth signs, we can tailor soil mixtures and nutrient regimes to enhance cannabis cultivation:

1. **Soil Mixtures:**
   - For Taurus energies, create a rich, loamy soil mix with plenty of organic matter that promotes moisture retention and fertility.
   - Under Virgo's influence, the soil should be fine and loose, allowing for excellent aeration and drainage. Adding sand or perlite can improve the texture and prevent compaction.
   - With Capricorn's aspect, integrate rock dust and bone meal to enhance the mineral content, supporting robust root systems and structural growth.
2. **Nutrient Regimes:**
   - During Taurus phases, focus on balanced N-P-K (Nitrogen, Phosphorus, Potassium) fertilizers that promote lush vegetative growth.
   - In Virgo phases, utilize micronutrient supplements to fine-tune the nutritional profile, ensuring that the plants receive all necessary trace elements for optimal health.
   - Capricorn periods are ideal for applying slow-release fertilizers that support long-term growth, especially useful during the vegetative stage of cannabis.

Case Studies and Historical Insights

To illustrate the effectiveness of these practices, we look at various historical and modern case studies where the alignment of soil preparation with earth signs has led to successful cannabis cultivation:

- A historical account from an ancient agricultural text describes how farmers observed the moon in Capricorn to determine the best days for adding lime and rock minerals to their fields, which improved the sturdiness of their crops.
- A modern-day organic cannabis farm in Northern California aligns its composting and soil amendment schedules with the phases of Taurus, resulting in a notable increase in the yield and potency of their harvest.
- In Colorado, a grower specializing in medicinal cannabis uses the Virgo period to meticulously adjust soil pH and composition, leading to a crop praised for its exceptional medicinal qualities.

By integrating these astrological principles with practical soil science, cultivators can create a harmonized and energetically balanced growing environment. This chapter not only equips you with the knowledge of how to prepare your soil in alignment with the earth signs but also inspires you to apply these practices to achieve tangible improvements in the health and yield of your cannabis plants. As we continue our journey through "Cosmic Cannabis Cultivation," the subsequent chapters will build on this foundation, exploring how celestial timing can guide every aspect of your cultivation process.

Check out my Virtual dispensary for all your hemp needs: https://shift.store/sg1fan23477/retail

Chapter 3: Germination and Early Growth - Water Signs Cancer, Scorpio, Pisces

Germination and early plant growth are critical phases in the life cycle of cannabis, requiring careful attention to moisture, temperature, and environmental energies. Water signs—Cancer, Scorpio, and Pisces—play a significant role in this stage, influencing how water interacts with cannabis seeds and seedlings to promote vigorous and healthy growth. This chapter explores the mystical and practical applications of water sign energies in the germination and early growth stages of cannabis, including innovative lunar watering techniques and spiritual rituals that enhance the vitality of young plants.

WATER'S ROLE IN CANNABIS CULTIVATION: INFLUENCE OF WATER SIGNS

Water signs bring intuition, emotional depth, and a strong connection to the fluidic aspects of the natural world. Their influence is particularly potent in enhancing the moisture-related processes essential for seed germination and early growth.

- **Cancer**: Ruled by the Moon, Cancer deeply affects water retention and absorption. Its influence is ideal for initiating germination, where consistent moisture levels are crucial. Aligning seed soaking and initial watering with the Cancer phase helps ensure that seeds receive gentle, nurturing energy, promoting robust sprouting.
- **Scorpio**: Governed by Pluto and Mars, Scorpio brings transformational energy that can enhance root development and the efficient uptake of nutrients from water. This sign is ideal for the early stages of root growth, where the establishment of a strong root system is critical for the absorption of water and nutrients.

- **Pisces**: Ruled by Neptune, Pisces is associated with nutrient diffusion and overall plant health in watery environments. Its influence is beneficial during the misting of seedlings, helping to create a supportive, humid environment that encourages tender young plants to thrive.

LUNAR WATERING TECHNIQUES

The phases of the moon not only influence the tides but also the water content in soil and plants. By syncing your watering schedule with the lunar cycle, you can optimize water usage and improve the health and growth rate of your cannabis plants.

1. **New Moon to First Quarter (Waxing Crescent)**: Begin increasing watering as the moon's gravitational pull starts drawing water upward. This phase is ideal for moisture absorption by young roots, encouraging strong and healthy growth.
2. **First Quarter to Full Moon (Waxing Gibbous)**: Maximize watering during this phase when the moon's pull is strongest, ensuring that plants are well-hydrated and prepared for the intense growth period that follows.
3. **Full Moon to Last Quarter (Waning Gibbous)**: Gradually reduce watering as the moon's influence lessens, allowing plants to process and utilize the stored moisture and nutrients efficiently.
4. **Last Quarter to New Moon (Waning Crescent)**: Minimize watering during this phase to encourage roots to grow deeper in search of moisture, strengthening the plant's foundation.

SPIRITUAL RITUALS FOR SPROUTING

Incorporating spiritual rituals into the germination and early growth stages can harness the emotional and mystical energies of the water signs, fostering an environment of growth and vitality:

- **Cancer Ritual**: During the new moon in Cancer, perform a ritual that involves watering your seeds with moon-charged water. Leave water out during the new moon night to absorb lunar energies, then use this water to moisten your seeds or soil, infusing them with Cancer's nurturing qualities.
- **Scorpio Ritual**: As seedlings begin to develop roots, use a Scorpio moon to chant or meditate on transformation and growth. Visualize the roots penetrating deeply and absorbing all the necessary nutrients, empowered by Scorpio's transformative energy.
- **Pisces Ritual**: When your seedlings are ready for a more humid environment, use a fine mist sprayer during a Pisces moon. Add a few drops of seaweed extract to the water to enhance nutrient intake and chant or sing to infuse the water with Piscean healing vibrations.

This chapter equips you with the knowledge and techniques to effectively integrate the energies of water signs into your cannabis cultivation practice. By understanding and applying these celestial influences, you ensure that your cannabis plants have the best possible start, setting the stage for a fruitful and potent harvest. As we continue to explore the interactions of astrological elements with cannabis cultivation, you will discover how to seamlessly integrate cosmic wisdom into every phase of your gardening efforts.

Check out my Virtual dispensary for all your hemp needs: https://shift.store/sg1fan23477/retail

Chapter 4: Vegetative Growth - Air Signs Gemini, Libra, Aquarius

The vegetative stage of cannabis cultivation is a period of rapid growth and development, where plants stretch out and expand in preparation for flowering. The air element, represented by the signs of Gemini, Libra, and Aquarius, plays a pivotal role in this phase, influencing how plants breathe, communicate, and respond to their environment. This chapter explores how harnessing the characteristics of air signs can promote vigorous vegetative growth, improve pruning and training practices, and enhance the plant's ability to adapt to and communicate within its surroundings.

HARNESSING THE AIR ELEMENT: LEVERAGING AIR SIGNS FOR VIGOROUS VEGETATIVE GROWTH

Air signs are associated with movement, flexibility, and exchange of ideas. In the context of cannabis cultivation, they influence the atmospheric conditions around the plants, which are critical for maintaining optimal growth rates and health during the vegetative stage.

- **Gemini**: Ruled by Mercury, Gemini brings a dynamic energy that can enhance the exchange of gases around the plant, particularly carbon dioxide absorption and oxygen release during photosynthesis. Cultivators can harness this energy by optimizing their ventilation systems and ensuring that plants are exposed to fresh, moving air, mimicking the stimulating effects of natural breezes.
- **Libra**: Governed by Venus, Libra's influence promotes balance and harmony within the plant's environment. This sign enhances the plant's ability to maintain homeostasis despite changes in environmental conditions. During the Libra phases, focus on adjusting the environmental factors such as humidity, light, and

temperature to ensure they are in perfect balance, facilitating uniform growth.

- **Aquarius**: Ruled by Uranus, Aquarius introduces an innovative and somewhat erratic energy that can stimulate rapid growth spurts. This sign encourages cultivators to experiment with new technologies in air management, like advanced air filtration systems or CO2 enrichment practices, to boost growth and vitality.

PRUNING AND TRAINING WITH THE WIND: TECHNIQUES ALIGNED WITH AIR SIGN DYNAMICS

Pruning and training are essential techniques used during the vegetative phase to control the shape and size of the cannabis plants, directing their energy into producing a more desirable structure for light exposure and air circulation.

- **Gemini Techniques**: Implementing multiple pruning sessions that are light and frequent aligns with Gemini's mutable and flexible nature. This approach encourages the plant to grow denser and bushier, which can lead to a more productive flowering stage.

- **Libra Techniques**: Training techniques like Low-Stress Training (LST) or the Screen of Green (ScrOG) are well-suited to Libra's balancing qualities. These methods involve gently bending and tying down branches to create an even canopy, which optimizes light distribution and air circulation around all parts of the plant.

- **Aquarius Techniques**: High-Stress Training (HST) techniques, such as topping or supercropping, can be aligned with Aquarius's innovative and radical energy. These methods involve creating controlled damage to the plant (like pinching or bending) to encourage it to grow more vigorously and resiliently.

ENHANCING PLANT COMMUNICATION: AIR-SIGN INFLUENCE ON ENVIRONMENTAL CONDITIONS

Air signs also influence the subtle ways plants communicate with their environment and with each other, particularly through airborne chemical signals.

- **Gemini's Impact**: Enhancing communication by optimizing spacing between plants to ensure that each one has enough room to "breathe" and receive signals from its neighbors, thereby improving overall plant health and vigor.
- **Libra's Impact**: Maintaining environmental harmony so that plants can utilize their natural signaling mechanisms effectively, avoiding stress signals that can occur when conditions are unbalanced.
- **Aquarius's Impact**: Encouraging diversity in plant species and strains in the grow area, which can lead to a more dynamic exchange of signals and a healthier, more resilient crop.

By understanding and applying the principles of air signs during the vegetative stage, cultivators can create a more conducive growing environment that promotes health, vitality, and preparedness for the flowering stage. This chapter provides a comprehensive guide to integrating astrological insights with practical cultivation techniques, offering you the tools to nurture your cannabis plants in harmony with the cosmic winds.

Check out my Virtual dispensary for all your hemp needs: https://shift.store/sg1fan23477/retail

Chapter 5: Flowering - Fire Signs Aries, Leo, Sagittarius

The flowering stage is a critical phase in the life cycle of cannabis, where buds form and mature, heralding the approach of harvest. Fire signs—Aries, Leo, and Sagittarius—symbolize energy, passion, and dynamism, traits that can significantly influence and enhance the flowering process. This chapter explores how the vibrant and intense energy of fire signs can be utilized to maximize the flowering potential of cannabis, focusing on specific adjustments in lighting and temperature, as well as incorporating energetic practices that promote robust and potent blooms.

Igniting Flowering with Fire: Influence of Fire Signs on Flowering

The fiery energy of Aries, Leo, and Sagittarius brings warmth and vitality, which are essential for the flowering stage. Each of these signs contributes uniquely to the development and maturation of cannabis flowers:

- **Aries**: Ruled by Mars, Aries injects a vigorous growth energy into plants, speeding up metabolism and increasing the rate of photosynthesis. This sign's influence is especially beneficial at the onset of the flowering stage, encouraging rapid initial floral development.
- **Leo**: Governed by the Sun, Leo enhances the plant's overall vitality and its capacity to produce larger, more resinous buds. Leo's sunny disposition promotes not just physical growth but also an increase in the plant's production of cannabinoids and terpenes, leading to higher potency and better flavor profiles.
- **Sagittarius**: Ruled by Jupiter, Sagittarius expands whatever it touches. In the context of cannabis, it can help increase the size and number of buds, as well as enhance the general health and resilience of the plant during the taxing flowering phase.

Lighting and Temperature Considerations: Adjusting Grow Lights and Environmental Controls

Proper lighting and temperature control are pivotal during the flowering stage. Aligning these factors with the energetic qualities of fire signs can lead to more successful outcomes:

- **Lighting Adjustments**:
  - During Aries, increase light intensity to mimic the added energy of this sign, promoting stronger and quicker bud development.
  - In Leo, consider using lights with a broader spectrum, particularly emphasizing the red end, which encourages budding and can lead to denser, more potent flowers.
  - As Sagittarius influences expansion, ensure that your lighting setup uniformly covers all plants, allowing each bud to receive ample light, minimizing popcorn buds (under-developed flowers).
- **Temperature Controls**:
  - Aries calls for slightly higher temperatures, mimicking early summer conditions which invigorate plant metabolism.
  - During Leo, maintain a warm and stable environment that mirrors mid-summer conditions, optimal for cannabinoid synthesis.
  - In Sagittarius, slightly decrease the temperature to prepare plants for the final push and to enhance the colors and resin production in the buds.

Energetic Practices for Bloom Enhancement: Rituals and Energetic Practices

Incorporating rituals and energetic practices during the flowering phase can align the plants with the cosmic energy of fire signs, fostering a more vibrant and potent bloom:

- **Aries Rituals**: Perform energizing and stimulating rituals at the beginning of the flowering phase. Light red candles around your grow space to invoke Aries' fiery energy, and use affirmations that focus on vigor and abundance.
- **Leo Rituals**: During Leo, create a ritual that celebrates the sun's energy. Use gold or yellow crystals like citrine or tiger's eye in your grow room to amplify Leo's solar energies, enhancing the life force of the plants.
- **Sagittarius Rituals**: Incorporate expansion-focused rituals in Sagittarius. Burn sage to clear the negative energy and encourage positive growth, and use rich, expansive scents like frankincense to promote the generous nature of Sagittarius.

By understanding and utilizing the characteristics of fire signs during the flowering stage, cultivators can significantly enhance the energy, potency, and yield of their cannabis plants. This chapter provides a blend of practical and mystical advice, offering you a comprehensive toolkit for maximizing the flowering potential of your crop in alignment with the dynamic and powerful energy of the fire signs. As we continue exploring the influence of cosmic elements in cannabis cultivation, your understanding of these synergies will deepen, enabling you to optimize each stage of growth for the best possible harvest.

Check out my Virtual dispensary for all your hemp needs: https://shift.store/sg1fan23477/retail

Chapter 6: Harvesting Under the Moon

Harvesting cannabis is the culmination of months of careful cultivation, where timing and technique significantly influence the final quality, potency, and medicinal properties of the buds. The moon, with its profound influence on all living things, plays a critical role during this phase. This chapter explores the art of lunar harvesting, providing insights into how the moon's phases and its position in the zodiac can optimize the harvest of cannabis. We also delve into the crucial pre-harvest rituals and preparations that set the stage for an effective cure.

LUNAR HARVESTING: CHOOSING THE RIGHT MOON PHASE

The phases of the moon impact the flow of moisture in plants and the earth, making certain times more optimal for harvesting cannabis to maximize the plant's medicinal qualities and overall potency:

- **Full Moon**: The gravitational pull is at its strongest, and the sap is at its highest point in the plants. Harvesting during the full moon maximizes the amount of active compounds like THC and CBD in the buds. This phase is considered ideal for achieving the most potent and aromatic cannabis.
- **Waning Moon**: As the moon wanes, the sap starts to recede back into the roots, which is good for plants that need to heal and restore after the harvest. This phase is suitable for harvesting plants intended for smoother, more mellow effects, as the decrease in sap lessens the intensity of the psychoactive properties.
- **New Moon**: Harvesting during the new moon is less common but can be ideal for specific medicinal purposes, particularly when lower potency is desired. The plant's energies are at their lowest, which can be suitable for producing cannabis with more subdued effects.

SIGN-SPECIFIC HARVESTING TIPS: HOW THE MOON'S SIGN AFFECTS HARVESTING

The zodiac sign in which the moon resides during harvesting also affects the quality and characteristics of the cannabis:

- **Water Signs (Cancer, Scorpio, Pisces)**: These signs are associated with moisture and healing properties. Harvesting during these signs is ideal for cannabis that will be used for its medicinal properties, enhancing its healing effects.
- **Earth Signs (Taurus, Virgo, Capricorn)**: Harvesting when the moon is in an earth sign helps enhance the density and weight of the buds, ideal for commercial cultivation where yield is a priority.
- **Air Signs (Gemini, Libra, Aquarius)**: These signs can enhance the aromatic properties of the buds. Harvest during these signs if the goal is to produce a fragrant crop with subtle effects.
- **Fire Signs (Aries, Leo, Sagittarius)**: Harvesting during fire signs can increase the potency and energizing effects of the cannabis, suitable for recreational strains intended for more stimulating experiences.

PREPARING FOR THE CURE: PRE-HARVEST RITUALS AND PREPARATIONS

The transition from harvesting to curing is crucial for preserving and enhancing the flavor, aroma, and potency of cannabis. Pre-harvest rituals and preparations can align the crop with cosmic energies, enhancing the effectiveness of the curing process:

- **Pre-Harvest Flushing**: Two weeks before the anticipated harvest, begin flushing the plants with plain water. This practice, aligned with the waning moon, helps remove excess nutrients and salts from the soil and plant tissues, improving the purity and smoothness of the final product.

- **Harvest Rituals**: On the day of harvest, consider performing a ritual to thank the plants for their growth and yield. This might involve meditating in the grow space, burning sage to clear negative energies, and expressing gratitude aloud. Aligning this ritual with the moon's energy can deepen your connection to the plants and enhance the spiritual quality of the harvest.
- **Moon Water**: Prepare moon water by leaving water exposed under the moonlight during the full moon. Use this water to moisten the scissors or shears before harvesting, infusing the process with lunar energy, which is believed to enhance the plant's energetic qualities.

This chapter provides a comprehensive guide to harvesting cannabis under the influence of the moon, from choosing the right phase to conducting sign-specific harvests and preparing for the cure. By understanding and utilizing these lunar dynamics, you can significantly influence the quality and characteristics of your cannabis, ensuring a harvest that is potent, flavorful, and aligned with cosmic rhythms. As you move forward in "Cosmic Cannabis Cultivation", these insights will help you to master the art of lunar harvesting, contributing to a holistic and spiritually fulfilling cultivation experience.

Check out my Virtual dispensary for all your hemp needs: https://shift.store/sg1fan23477/retail

Chapter 7: Curing and Storing - Aligning with Cosmic Rhythms

The post-harvest processes of curing and storing cannabis are crucial for developing and preserving the aromatic, flavorful, and psychoactive properties of the buds. This chapter explores how celestial bodies and cosmic rhythms can influence these critical phases, offering insights into aligning these processes with astrological events to maximize the quality and potency of your cannabis. We also delve into the methods of storing cannabis that help maintain its cosmic energy and potency over time.

Celestial Curing: Influences of Celestial Bodies on the Curing Process

Curing cannabis involves carefully controlled drying of the harvested buds to ensure the breakdown of chlorophyll and the preservation of cannabinoids and terpenes. The influence of celestial bodies, particularly the moon and planets, can enhance this process:

- **Lunar Influence**: The moon's phases can affect the moisture content in the atmosphere, which in turn influences the drying and curing of cannabis. Aligning the start of the curing process with the waning moon, when atmospheric moisture is decreasing, can help reduce the risk of mold and speed up the drying process without sacrificing the quality of volatile compounds like terpenes.

- **Planetary Influence**: Planets can also affect the curing process through their metaphysical properties:
    - **Mercury** (communication) can be considered to enhance the interaction between the chemical components of the buds, improving the breakdown of sugars and chlorophyll.
    - **Venus** (harmony) supports the preservation of flavors and aromas, making it ideal for curing processes aimed at enhancing taste and smell.

○ **Saturn** (structure) can be invoked to aid in the preservation of the physical integrity of the buds during curing, ensuring they do not crumble or become overly dry.

Astrological Timing for Curing: Best Practices for Timing the Curing Process

The timing of the curing process can be optimized by considering astrological events:

- **Zodiacal Influence**: The zodiac sign in which the moon and other planets are located can influence the qualities emphasized during curing. For instance:
  ○ Curing during a moon in **Earth signs** (Taurus, Virgo, Capricorn) can help preserve the weight and density of the buds.
  ○ A moon in **Water signs** (Cancer, Scorpio, Pisces) is ideal for maintaining moisture balance, ensuring the buds do not dry out too quickly or retain too much water.
  ○ **Air signs** (Gemini, Libra, Aquarius) are favorable for enhancing the aroma profiles during the curing phase, facilitating better air flow and exchange within the curing environment.
- **Planetary Transits**: Aligning curing starts with favorable planetary transits can enhance specific qualities in the cannabis. For instance, starting the cure when Venus transits a favorable sign can enhance the sensory properties of the buds, such as flavor and aroma.

Storage and Cosmic Energies: How to Store Cannabis to Maintain Its Cosmic Energy and Potency

Proper storage is essential to preserve the quality and energetic properties of cannabis after curing. Here are some tips for storing your cannabis in a way that maintains its cosmic energies:

- **Container Materials**: Use materials that resonate with cosmic energies. Glass jars are excellent for storing cannabis as they do not react chemically with the contents and can be easily sealed to maintain freshness. Colored glass, such as violet or amber, can also be used to filter out harmful UV rays while allowing beneficial light frequencies to enhance the energy of the stored cannabis.
- **Environmental Considerations**: Store your cannabis in a cool, dark, and dry place to preserve its potency. Aligning your storage area with Feng Shui principles or Vastu Shastra can further enhance the cosmic harmony and energy preservation of the space.
- **Energetic Charging**: Consider storing your cannabis under a pyramid structure or placing crystals such as quartz or amethyst in the storage area to charge the buds with positive energy. Periodically exposing the stored cannabis to moonlight during full moons can also recharge its vibrational energy.

By understanding and applying these celestial and astrological principles, you can effectively align the curing and storage of your cannabis with cosmic rhythms, enhancing not only the physical quality but also the energetic potency of your harvest. This chapter provides you with the tools and knowledge needed to preserve and amplify the cosmic energies imbued in your cannabis, ensuring that every aspect of your cultivation process is harmonized with the greater workings of the universe.

Check out my Virtual dispensary for all your hemp needs: https://shift.store/sg1fan23477/retail

Chapter 8: Cosmic Pest and Disease Management

Effective pest and disease management is crucial for maintaining the health and productivity of cannabis crops. By integrating cosmic wisdom and celestial influences, cultivators can enhance traditional pest management techniques with planetary protection, lunar timing, and spiritual energy shields. This chapter delves into the innovative integration of these elements, providing a holistic approach to protecting cannabis crops from common pests and diseases.

PLANETARY PROTECTION: NATURAL PEST AND DISEASE MANAGEMENT TECHNIQUES ALIGNED WITH PLANETARY POSITIONS

Planetary influences can be harnessed to enhance the natural resilience of cannabis plants against pests and diseases:

- **Mars**: The energy of Mars is associated with defense and aggression. Aligning pest management strategies with Mars can enhance the plants' natural ability to repel pests. For example, applying natural pesticides or introducing beneficial predators during Mars-aligned days can increase effectiveness and deterrence.

- **Saturn**: Known for its properties of restriction and protection, Saturn can help fortify plants against diseases. Implementing fungal and bacterial control measures when Saturn is prominently positioned can reinforce plant structures and immune responses.

- **Jupiter**: Jupiter's expansive nature can be beneficial for promoting plant health and vigor, making them less susceptible to pests and diseases. Enhancing soil fertility and plant nutrition during Jupiter transits ensures that plants are robust and better equipped to ward off ailments.

LUNAR PHASES AND PEST CONTROL: TIMING PEST CONTROL MEASURES WITH THE LUNAR CALENDAR

The phases of the moon significantly influence the life cycles of many insects and the physiological responses of plants, making lunar timing a strategic factor in pest and disease management:

- **New Moon to First Quarter (Waxing Crescent)**: This phase is ideal for applying organic growth-promoting inputs like compost teas and microbial inoculants that enhance plant health and resistance to pests and diseases.
- **First Quarter to Full Moon (Waxing Gibbous)**: As the moon waxes, plant sap flow increases, which can attract pests. This is an effective time to apply barrier methods and repellents to protect the plants when they are most vulnerable.
- **Full Moon to Last Quarter (Waning Gibbous)**: The full moon is a peak time for insect activity. Applying natural pesticides during this phase can catch pests at their most active, improving control efficiency.
- **Last Quarter to New Moon (Waning Crescent)**: As the moon wanes, it's an opportune time to clear away dead plant material and other debris that may harbor pests or diseases, reducing future outbreaks.

SPIRITUAL AND ENERGETIC SHIELDS: CREATING PROTECTIVE ENERGY BARRIERS USING COSMIC WISDOM

Beyond physical and biological methods, spiritual and energetic practices can create a protective aura around cannabis crops:

- **Energy Shielding Rituals**: Conducting rituals to invoke protective energies can be powerful. For instance, planting protective herbs like basil or lavender in accordance with specific planetary alignments (such as Mars for repelling negative energy) can create a natural energetic barrier.

- **Crystal Grids**: Setting up crystal grids around the garden using stones like black tourmaline for protection or shungite for purification can help shield the plants energetically. Aligning these setups during favorable planetary transits enhances their effectiveness.

- **Moon Water**: Spraying plants with moon water prepared during the full moon can imbue them with lunar energy, offering an additional layer of energetic protection. This practice can be especially potent when aiming to align with water-sign energies, known for their nurturing and protective qualities.

By integrating these cosmic and holistic approaches, cultivators can manage pests and diseases more effectively while maintaining the natural balance and harmony of their cannabis gardens. This chapter provides a comprehensive guide to using celestial forces for pest and disease management, ensuring that your cultivation practices are not only effective but also aligned with the universal energies that influence all life forms.

Check out my Virtual dispensary for all your hemp needs: https://shift.store/sg1fan23477/retail

Chapter 9: Advanced Cosmic Techniques

As you advance in your journey of Cosmic Cannabis Cultivation, you can integrate more sophisticated techniques that fuse ancient wisdom with modern agricultural practices. This chapter introduces biodynamic cannabis cultivation, the use of planetary hours for timing cultivation activities, and astrological companion planting. These methods will deepen your connection to the cosmic energies and enhance the effectiveness of your cannabis cultivation.

BIODYNAMIC CANNABIS CULTIVATION: INTEGRATING BIODYNAMIC FARMING PRINCIPLES

Biodynamic agriculture is an advanced form of organic farming that treats farms as unified and individual organisms, emphasizing the interrelationship between soil health, plants, and animals in a self-sustaining system. This approach includes the use of cosmic rhythms to guide farming activities.

- **Preparations**: Biodynamic cannabis cultivation involves specific preparations made from mineral, plant, or animal manure extracts, buried in the ground in cow horns for six months, then used very diluted to energize the soil and plants. These preparations help harness terrestrial and celestial forces to promote soil fertility and plant health.
- **Cosmic Calendar**: The biodynamic sowing and planting calendar, which considers moon phases and astrological constellations, is crucial. For instance, root development is enhanced when the moon is in an earth sign, while flowering is best supported when in a water sign, aligning these phases with cannabis cultivation cycles for optimal growth and potency.

PLANETARY HOURS FOR PLANT WORK: SELECTING THE MOST AUSPICIOUS TIMES

Planetary hours are segments of time in the day, each ruled by a different planet, according to ancient astrological principles. Each hour carries the energy of its ruling planet, influencing various types of activities, including cannabis cultivation:

- **Calculating Planetary Hours**: To determine the planetary hours, you divide the time between sunrise and sunset into 12 equal parts; each part is an hour long and ruled by a specific planet in a sequence that changes daily. This cycle influences when to plant, prune, or harvest for enhancing the plants' vibrational qualities.
- **Application in Cultivation**: For example, hours ruled by Saturn are good for pruning to enhance plant structure, while Jupiter's hours might be chosen for transplanting to promote growth and expansion. Aligning these tasks with the planetary hours can maximize the effectiveness of each action and enhance the health and yield of the cannabis plants.

ASTROLOGICAL COMPANION PLANTING: USING THE ZODIAC TO GUIDE COMPANION PLANTING FOR CANNABIS

Companion planting is a method used to enhance garden health and productivity by placing plants together that mutually benefit each other, either by deterring pests, enhancing growth, or improving flavor. Astrology can guide this process by aligning plant associations with zodiac signs:

- **Zodiac Characteristics and Plant Traits**: Each zodiac sign governs specific plant characteristics. For example, Aries rules plants that are typically high in iron, such as spinach, which can be beneficial to the soil quality for cannabis. Taurus governs over luxurious, leafy plants which might help shade cannabis plants lightly without overshadowing them.

- **Astrological Benefits**: Companion planting according to astrological signs can also optimize pest management and improve pollination. For instance, Gemini rules air-sign plants that might help improve air circulation around the cannabis plants, reducing mold and mildew risks.

- **Practical Implementation**: Planting marigolds, governed by Leo, around cannabis can deter pests, while basil, under Scorpio's rule, may help improve the oil and flavor profile of cannabis buds. These companions are selected based on their astrological associations and practical benefits, creating a harmonious and beneficial plant ecosystem.

By applying these advanced cosmic techniques, you can take your Cosmic Cannabis Cultivation to new heights, creating a deeply interconnected and energetically aligned garden. This holistic approach not only enhances the growth and potency of your cannabis but also contributes to a sustainable and spiritually enriching farming practice.

Check out my Virtual dispensary for all your hemp needs: https://shift.store/sg1fan23477/retail

Chapter 10: Cosmic Cannabis and Community

In the journey of Cosmic Cannabis Cultivation, the final and perhaps most fulfilling aspect involves integrating the community into the cultivation process. This chapter delves into how the fruits of your cosmic cultivation efforts can be shared and celebrated within a community, strengthening bonds and spreading the holistic and spiritual benefits of cannabis grown under cosmic influences. We explore sharing the harvest, hosting cosmic cannabis ceremonies, and teaching cosmic cultivation practices.

SHARING THE HARVEST: BUILDING COMMUNITY AND SHARING CANNABIS GROWN UNDER BENEFICIAL COSMIC CONDITIONS

Sharing the harvest goes beyond mere distribution of cannabis—it's about fostering a community spirit and acknowledging the collective energies that contribute to the cultivation process. Here's how to effectively share your cosmic cannabis:

- **Community Supported Agriculture (CSA) Models**: Setting up a CSA for cannabis allows community members to buy into the harvest early in the season, and in return, they receive a portion of the cannabis yield. This model supports the cultivator financially and creates a direct connection between the grower and the community.
- **Cannabis Co-ops**: Establishing or joining a cannabis cooperative can enhance resource sharing, from cultivation to distribution. This setup encourages a communal approach to growing cannabis where techniques, seeds, and experiences are shared.
- **Sharing as Ritual**: Organize harvest sharing days with a focus on gratitude and cosmic appreciation. Encourage community members to participate in the final harvesting and initial processing phases. This inclusion helps demystify the process and

educates people about the importance of cosmic alignments in cultivation.

COSMIC CANNABIS CEREMONIES: HOSTING CEREMONIES TO CELEBRATE THE HARVEST AND HONOR THE COSMIC FORCES

Ceremonies can transform the harvest process into a spiritual event, acknowledging the cosmic forces at play and the communal effort in cultivation:

- **Planning the Ceremony**: Align the ceremony with significant celestial events, such as the autumn equinox or a full moon. These times hold particular power and can enhance the spiritual experience of the ceremony.

- **Activities During the Ceremony**: Include drum circles, guided meditations, and shared testimonials of the personal journeys through cosmic cultivation. Use these activities to deepen the connection between the participants and the cosmic energies.

- **Ceremonial Consumption**: Prepare and share cannabis in ways that honor its sacred nature. This might include creating special cannabis-infused foods or herbal blends that highlight the plant's medicinal and spiritual properties, consumed in a mindful, communal setting.

TEACHING COSMIC CULTIVATION: SPREADING KNOWLEDGE ABOUT COSMIC CANNABIS CULTIVATION PRACTICES

Educating others about the benefits and techniques of cosmic cannabis cultivation ensures the longevity and spread of these practices:

- **Workshops and Classes**: Organize educational sessions that cover the basics of cosmic cultivation, from understanding the celestial influences to practical gardening tips. These can be held at local community centers, online, or through local gardening clubs.

- **Mentorship Programs**: Develop a mentorship program where experienced cosmic cultivators guide newcomers through their first growing season. This hands-on approach helps to instill confidence and pass on nuanced knowledge that might not be captured in written guides.
- **Creation of Written and Digital Content**: Write articles, blogs, or even books about your experiences and insights gained from cosmic cannabis cultivation. Producing video content that shows the step-by-step processes can also help reach a broader audience.

By embracing the community aspect of cosmic cannabis cultivation, you not only enrich your own experience but also contribute to a larger movement towards sustainable and spiritually aware cannabis cultivation practices. This chapter provides a blueprint for integrating community, spirituality, and education into your cosmic cannabis journey, promoting a holistic approach that benefits all involved.

Check out my Virtual dispensary for all your hemp needs: https://shift.store/sg1fan23477/retail

Conclusion: From the Soil to the Stars

As we conclude our journey through "Cosmic Cannabis Cultivation," we reflect on the profound interconnectedness between the cosmos and cannabis cultivation. This exploration has not only revealed the potential for enhancing the growth, potency, and medicinal qualities of cannabis but has also offered a deeper understanding of the rhythms and energies that govern all forms of life. Here, we summarize the transformative impact of cosmic cultivation, encourage ongoing exploration and growth, and speculate on the future frontiers in this unique cultivation method.

REFLECTING ON THE JOURNEY: SUMMARIZING THE COSMIC CANNABIS CULTIVATION JOURNEY

Throughout this book, we have navigated the celestial influences that play a pivotal role in every stage of the cannabis life cycle—from preparing the soil under the guidance of earth signs to harvesting by the lunar cycles. Each chapter has provided insights into how integrating cosmic principles can significantly enhance the cultivation process, benefiting both the grower and the plant.

For the grower, this journey offers more than just a method to improve crop yields; it is a path to spiritual and environmental harmony, bringing the cultivator closer to the natural world and its cosmic energies. For the cannabis plant, the application of these celestial techniques means growth in an environment that respects and utilizes the universal forces, resulting in a product that is not only superior in quality but also rich in energetic properties.

THE INFINITE CYCLE OF GROWTH: ENCOURAGING CONTINUAL EXPLORATION AND INTEGRATION

The principles of cosmic cannabis cultivation are dynamic, mirroring the ever-evolving nature of the cosmos itself. As growers, the invitation is to continue exploring these cosmic connections, experimenting with new techniques, and refining existing practices in tune with personal observations and cosmic rhythms.

- **Seasonal Adaptation**: Each growing season offers new insights and opportunities for applying cosmic principles differently. Observe how changes in celestial configurations affect your cultivation outcomes and adapt your practices accordingly.
- **Community Learning**: Engage with a community of fellow cosmic cultivators to exchange knowledge, experiences, and innovations. Community gardens, online forums, and workshops can be invaluable resources for shared learning and support.
- **Personal Growth**: As you integrate these practices, reflect on your personal growth. Cosmic cultivation is as much about growing as a person as it is about cultivating cannabis. The patience, attentiveness, and connection to the natural and cosmic cycles are profound teachings that extend beyond agriculture.

FUTURE FRONTIERS IN COSMIC CANNABIS: SPECULATING ON INNOVATIONS AND RESEARCH

Looking ahead, the field of cosmic cannabis cultivation holds promising potential for new research and innovations:

- **Scientific Exploration**: As interest in holistic and astrological influences on agriculture grows, scientific studies could explore the quantifiable effects of lunar and planetary alignments on plant growth. This research can help validate and refine cosmic cultivation practices, making them more accessible and tailored to different environments and climates.
- **Technological Integration**: Technology that aligns with cosmic cycles, such as biodynamically calibrated growing systems, could automate and optimize the timing of watering, feeding, and light exposure based on astrological calendars. This fusion

of ancient wisdom and modern technology would further revolutionize cosmic cannabis cultivation.

- **Expanding the Scope**: Beyond cannabis, the principles discussed in this book could inspire similar approaches in the cultivation of other crops, potentially leading to a broader movement towards cosmic farming practices that could benefit global agricultural practices.

In conclusion, "Cosmic Cannabis Cultivation" is more than a manual; it is a manifesto for a deeper, more harmonious engagement with the forces of nature and the cosmos. As you continue to apply these insights, may your cultivation not only yield abundant harvests but also contribute to a greater understanding and respect for the celestial influences that enrich our world. From the soil to the stars, the journey of cosmic cannabis cultivation is an infinite cycle of growth and discovery.

Appendix: Resources for Cosmic Cannabis Cultivation

This appendix serves as a comprehensive guide to resources for cultivators interested in exploring and applying cosmic principles to cannabis cultivation. From books and online courses to tools and community networks, these resources will provide you with the knowledge and support needed to deepen your understanding of cosmic cannabis cultivation.

BOOKS AND LITERATURE

1. **"The Biodynamic Farm" by Herbert Koepf** - Offers insights into biodynamic farming principles that can be applied to cannabis cultivation.

2. **"Lunar and Biodynamic Gardening" by Matthew Jackson** - Provides practical tips on planting, sowing, and harvesting in alignment with the lunar calendar.

3. **"Secrets of the Zodiac" by Michele Finey** - Explores the deeper meanings of astrological signs and planetary influences that can be integrated into cultivation practices.

4. **"Astrological Gardening: The Ancient Wisdom of Successful Planting & Harvesting by the Stars" by Louise Riotte** - A guide to using astrological information to enhance garden planning and maintenance.

ONLINE RESOURCES AND COURSES

1. **The Biodynamic Association Website** - Offers courses, webinars, and articles on biodynamic agriculture techniques.
   - Website: Biodynamic Association

2. **Astro.com** - Provides detailed astrological charts and planetary calendars that can be customized for agricultural purposes.
   - Website: Astro.com

3. **Rudolf Steiner Archive** - An online repository of lectures and writings by Rudolf Steiner, the founder of biodynamic farming.

  ○ Website: Rudolf Steiner Archive
4. **Lunar Planting Calendar and Astrological Viewers** - Various gardening websites offer lunar planting calendars tailored to help gardeners schedule their planting and harvesting according to the moon phases.
  ○ Example: The Gardening Calendar

TOOLS FOR COSMIC CULTIVATION

1. **Lunar Phase Calendars** - Essential for tracking the phases of the moon and planning activities around them.
2. **Astrological Planting Charts** - These charts help identify the best times for planting, transplanting, pruning, and harvesting based on astrological conditions.
3. **Biodynamic Preparations** - Resources for obtaining or making the biodynamic preparations used in this type of agriculture.
4. **Soil Testing Kits** - Useful for determining soil composition and health, aligning soil amendment practices with cosmic rhythms.

COMMUNITY NETWORKS AND FORUMS

1. **Biodynamic Farming and Gardening Association** - A community of practitioners who share knowledge and experiences in biodynamic agriculture.
  ○ Website: Biodynamic Association
2. **Online Forums such as Reddit and Cannabis Cultivation Boards** - Places where growers share experiences and advice on cosmic and traditional cultivation techniques.
  ○ Example: r/microgrowery
3. **Local Gardening Clubs and Meetups** - Engaging with local clubs can provide hands-on experience and mentoring in biodynamic and cosmic cannabis cultivation.

WORKSHOPS, CONFERENCES, AND SYMPOSIUMS

1. **Annual Biodynamic Conference** - A gathering that offers workshops, lectures, and networking opportunities focused on biodynamic practices.
2. **Astrological Associations' Annual Meetings** - Events that often include sessions on agricultural astrology and its practical applications.

These resources are intended to support both novice and experienced cultivators in their quest to integrate cosmic principles into their cannabis cultivation practices. By engaging with these materials and communities, you can expand your knowledge, refine your techniques, and contribute to the evolving field of cosmic cannabis cultivation.

Appendix B: Differences Between Male and Female Cannabis Plants

In the world of cannabis cultivation, understanding the differences between male and female plants is crucial for optimizing yield, potency, and quality. This appendix provides a detailed exploration of the physical and functional distinctions between male and female cannabis plants, offering insights that are essential for both novice and experienced growers.

BASIC BOTANICAL DIFFERENCES

Cannabis is a dioecious plant, meaning it produces male and female flowers on separate plants. However, monoecious plants, which produce both male and female flowers on the same plant, can also occur. The primary differences between male and female cannabis plants are:

- **Physical Appearance**: Male plants typically grow taller and thinner than their female counterparts. They develop fewer leaves and have a more rugged, less dense appearance. Female plants are usually bushier with more leaves and dense branching.
- **Flowers**: Male plants produce small, pollen-producing flowers that cluster in balls (pollen sacs), usually found at the leaf joints. Female plants produce larger, hairier flowers (buds) that are sticky to the touch due to the presence of trichomes, the glands that produce cannabinoids like THC and CBD.

IMPORTANCE OF SEX IN CULTIVATION

The sex of cannabis plants plays a significant role in cultivation for several reasons:

- **Seed Production**: Male plants are essential for breeding because their pollen is needed to fertilize female plants, which will then produce seeds. This is important for creating new strains or producing seeds for future crops.

- **Cannabinoid Content**: Female plants are generally more valuable to both recreational and medicinal users because they produce significantly higher levels of cannabinoids in their buds. Male plants contain some cannabinoids but in much lower concentrations.

- **Harvest Quality and Yield**: For most growers, especially those focused on producing consumable cannabis products, female plants are preferable. The presence of males can lead to fertilized females, which will focus their energy on producing seeds rather than developing potent and large buds.

IDENTIFYING MALE AND FEMALE PLANTS

Identifying the sex of cannabis plants early on is crucial for cultivation strategies, especially if the goal is to avoid seed production:

- **Pre-flowers**: From about 4 to 6 weeks of age, before entering the full flowering phase, cannabis plants start to show small structures known as pre-flowers at the nodes (where the leaves and branches extend from the stem). Male pre-flowers are small and round, while female pre-flowers are slightly pointed and will develop two hair-like structures called pistils that are usually white or orange.

- **Timing**: Male plants often show their sex earlier than female plants. Observing the growth patterns and pre-flower development can help determine the plant's sex before the flowering stage begins.

MANAGEMENT STRATEGIES

- **Separation**: In cannabis cultivation for flower production, male plants are typically separated from females to prevent pollination, unless breeding is intended. This separation should occur as soon as males are identified to ensure females remain unfertilized.

- **Culling**: Many growers choose to remove male plants from their gardens entirely to ensure that all energy is devoted to producing high-quality, seedless female flowers.
- **Utilization of Males**: Although less valuable for cannabinoid production, male plants can be used for other purposes such as fiber production or as a genetic resource in breeding programs.

ADVANCED TIPS FOR HANDLING MALE CANNABIS PLANTS

For cultivators interested in breeding or who need male plants for other purposes, managing their pollen for controlled fertilization is key. Collecting pollen in a controlled environment and storing it properly allows for specific breeding objectives without risking unwanted pollination of the entire crop.

CONCLUSION

Understanding the differences between male and female cannabis plants is essential for successful cultivation, especially in producing high-quality, potent cannabis flowers. By identifying and managing male and female plants appropriately, cultivators can optimize their operations to achieve the desired product quality and yield.

Appendix C: Cannabis Breeds and Strains Guide

This appendix provides a comprehensive guide to various cannabis breeds and strains, offering insights into their characteristics, cultivation requirements, and effects. Cannabis strains are bred to highlight specific traits, which can significantly influence their therapeutic benefits, growth patterns, and consumer preferences. Here, we will explore some of the most popular and medically beneficial cannabis strains, their genetic backgrounds, and unique attributes.

UNDERSTANDING CANNABIS GENETICS

Cannabis strains are typically categorized into three primary types based on their genetic lineage:

- **Indica**: Known for their bushy, short stature and broad leaves, indica strains generally produce relaxing and sedating effects, often recommended for nighttime use. They are particularly effective for pain relief, anxiety, and insomnia.
- **Sativa**: Characterized by their tall stature and narrow leaves, sativa strains usually provide an uplifting and energizing effect, making them suitable for daytime use. They are often prescribed for their ability to enhance creativity, increase focus, and combat depression.
- **Hybrid**: Hybrids are crosses between indica and sativa strains, designed to blend the characteristics of both parent strains. The effects can vary greatly depending on the specific parent strains used and their dominant traits.

POPULAR CANNABIS STRAINS

Here we discuss some key strains within each category, noting their effects, growing difficulty, and medicinal benefits.

Indica Strains

1. **Northern Lights**: One of the most famous indica strains, known for its fast flowering and resilience during growth. It typically brings on a comfortable laziness and relaxed euphoria, making it great for stress relief and sleep disorders.
2. **Granddaddy Purple**: Renowned for its distinctive berry and grape aroma, this strain is used medicinally to combat pain, muscle spasms, insomnia, and appetite loss.
3. **Blue Cheese**: This strain is known for its unique blueberry and cheese aroma, offering a relaxing and sedative effect that helps manage pain and muscle spasms.

Sativa Strains

1. **Green Crack**: Despite its intense name, Green Crack is appreciated for its sharp energy and focus. It induces an invigorating mental buzz that keeps you going throughout the day.
2. **Jack Herer**: Named after the cannabis activist, this strain combines a blissful cerebral high with a soothing body effect. It is often used for mental stress and depression.
3. **Sour Diesel**: A fast-acting strain that delivers energizing, dreamy cerebral effects. It has marked benefits for stress, pain, and depression.

Hybrid Strains

1. **OG Kush**: A highly popular strain that offers a powerful mix of head and body high, making it ideal for relaxation and pain relief.
2. **White Widow**: Famous for its potent buds covered in crystal resin, offering a powerful burst of euphoria and energy. It stimulates conversation and creativity.

3. **Blue Dream**: A relaxing yet stimulating hybrid that combines full-body relaxation with a gentle cerebral invigoration. It is popular among those treating pain, depression, and nausea.

CULTIVATION TIPS

Each strain has specific requirements for optimal growth:

- **Climate**: Sativa strains generally prefer warmer, more humid climates, while indicas thrive in cooler conditions. Hybrids can vary significantly based on their dominant traits.
- **Growing Difficulty**: Some strains, like Blue Dream, are relatively easy to grow and thus suitable for beginners, while others, like Sour Diesel, might require more experience due to their susceptibility to mold and pests.
- **Flowering Time**: Indicas typically have shorter flowering periods (6-8 weeks), making them faster to cultivate than sativas, which can take 9-12 weeks to flower. Hybrids will vary.

CONCLUSION

Understanding the nuances of different cannabis strains not only enhances a grower's ability to produce a desired crop but also enables users to better select a strain that aligns with their health and wellness goals. Whether for recreational enjoyment or medicinal relief, the diversity of cannabis strains offers a broad spectrum of therapeutic and experiential benefits. This guide serves as a starting point for cultivators and consumers alike to explore the rich genetic tapestry of cannabis.

Appendix D: Star Cannabis Horoscope

In this unique appendix, we explore the fascinating intersection of astrology and cannabis cultivation, providing a "Star Cannabis Horoscope." This guide offers insights into how cosmic forces, as understood through the signs of the zodiac, can influence both the growth of cannabis plants and the therapeutic effects they may offer. Each sign's influence is linked to specific cultivation tips and strain recommendations that align with the energetic qualities associated with that astrological sign.

ARIES (MARCH 21 - APRIL 19)

Cultivation Tips: Begin new projects with Aries' pioneering spirit —ideal for germinating seeds or starting new clones. Aries' fiery energy helps initiate rapid growth. **Strain Recommendation:** Sativa strains like Jack Herer, which energize and stimulate creativity, resonating with Aries' enthusiastic and dynamic nature.

TAURUS (APRIL 20 - MAY 20)

Cultivation Tips: Focus on soil enrichment as Taurus values stability and richness. This period is excellent for improving your growing medium. **Strain Recommendation:** Indica strains like Granddaddy Purple, which provide relaxation and sensory enhancement, mirroring Taurus' appreciation for comfort and luxury.

GEMINI (MAY 21 - JUNE 20)

Cultivation Tips: Engage in training techniques such as topping and pruning during Gemini's communicative air sign phase to promote plant conversation. **Strain Recommendation:** Hybrid strains like Blue Dream, which balance cerebral stimulation with physical relaxation, matching Gemini's dual nature.

CANCER (JUNE 21 - JULY 22)

Cultivation Tips: Optimize water usage; Cancer's water sign enhances moisture uptake and helps plants thrive during their vegetative growth phase. **Strain Recommendation:** Indica-dominant hybrids like Blue Cheese, which help manage stress and anxiety, reflecting Cancer's nurturing qualities.

LEO (JULY 23 - AUGUST 22)

Cultivation Tips: Increase light exposure to maximize growth potential during Leo's sunny disposition—ideal for the flowering phase. **Strain Recommendation:** Sativa strains like Super Lemon Haze, which uplift and invigorate, resonating with Leo's vibrant and theatrical spirit.

VIRGO (AUGUST 23 - SEPTEMBER 22)

Cultivation Tips: Focus on pest and disease management; Virgo's meticulous attention to detail helps in spotting early signs of trouble. **Strain Recommendation:** CBD-rich strains like ACDC, which offer medicinal benefits without psychoactive effects, aligning with Virgo's health-oriented approach.

LIBRA (SEPTEMBER 23 - OCTOBER 22)

Cultivation Tips: Balance nutrients and environmental factors to ensure even growth and plant health, reflecting Libra's need for harmony. **Strain Recommendation:** Balanced hybrids like White Widow, which provide an equal mind-body experience, suitable for Libra's quest for balance.

SCORPIO (OCTOBER 23 - NOVEMBER 21)

Cultivation Tips: Undertake deep water culture or hydroponics as Scorpio's transformative energy thrives in intense growing setups. **Strain Recommendation:** Potent strains like Gorilla Glue, known for its deep psychoactive effects, matching Scorpio's intense and mysterious nature.

SAGITTARIUS (NOVEMBER 22 - DECEMBER 21)

Cultivation Tips: Experiment with new cultivation techniques and exotic strains; Sagittarius' adventurous spirit encourages exploration. **Strain Recommendation:** Landrace sativas like Durban Poison, which stimulate and expand consciousness, reflecting Sagittarius' love for exploration.

CAPRICORN (DECEMBER 22 - JANUARY 19)

Cultivation Tips: Focus on structural support and maximizing yields through training methods, reflecting Capricorn's goal-oriented approach. **Strain Recommendation:** Traditional strains like Northern Lights, known for their reliability and high yields, align with Capricorn's pragmatic and disciplined nature.

AQUARIUS (JANUARY 20 - FEBRUARY 18)

Cultivation Tips: Implement advanced technologies like LED lighting or automated systems; Aquarius' innovative energy fosters technological integration. **Strain Recommendation:** Unique hybrid strains like Girl Scout Cookies, which offer novel flavors and effects, resonating with Aquarius' uniqueness.

PISCES (FEBRUARY 19 - MARCH 20)

Cultivation Tips: Enhance the spiritual aspect of your cultivation practice, perhaps through music or creative arts, during Pisces' dreamy phase. **Strain Recommendation:** Strains with high THC content like Purple Haze, which encourage deep introspection and relaxation, mirroring Pisces' mystical and introspective qualities.

This "Star Cannabis Horoscope" serves as a fun and engaging way to connect the cosmic influences of astrology with practical cannabis cultivation and strain selection, enhancing both the growing process and the enjoyment of its fruits. Whether you're a seasoned cultivator or a casual enthusiast, these insights offer an innovative layer to your cannabis experience.

-
-
-
-
-
-
-
-
-
-
-
-
-
-
-
-
-
-
-
-

<u>Message from the Author:</u>

I hope you enjoyed this book, I love astrology and knew there was not a book such as this out on the shelf. I love metaphysical items as well. Please check out my other books:

-Life of Government Benefits

-My life of Hell

-My life with Hydrocephalus

-Red Sky

-World Domination:Woman's rule

-World Domination:Woman's Rule 2: The War

-Life and Banishment of Apophis: book 1

-The Kidney Friendly Diet

-The Ultimate Hemp Cookbook

-Creating a Dispensary(legally)

-Cleanliness throughout life: the importance of showering from childhood to adulthood.

-Strong Roots: The Risks of Overcoddling children

-Hemp Horoscopes: Cosmic Insights and Earthly Healing

- Celestial Hemp Navigating the Zodiac: Through the Green Cosmos

-Astrological Hemp: Aligning The Stars with Earth's Ancient Herb

-The Astrological Guide to Hemp: Stars, Signs, and Sacred Leaves

-Green Growth: Innovative Marketing Strategies for your Hemp Products and Dispensary

-Cosmic Cannabis

-Astrological Munchies

-Henry The Hemp

-Zodiacal Roots: The Astrological Soul Of Hemp

- **Green Constellations: Intersection of Hemp and Zodiac**

-Hemp in The Houses: An astrological Adventure Through The Cannabis Galaxy

-Galactic Ganja Guide

Heavenly Hemp

Zodiac Leaves

Doctor Who Astrology

Cannastrology

Stellar Satvias and Cosmic Indicas

Celestial Cannabis: A Zodiac Journey

AstroHerbology: The Sky and The Soil: Volume 1

AstroHerbology:Celestial Cannabis:Volume 2

Check out my Virtual dispensary for all your hemp needs: https://shift.store/sg1fan23477/retail

If you want solar for your home go here: https://www.harborsolar.live/apophisenterprises/

Instagrams: @apophis_enterprises, @hempkingdom2024,

@apophisbookemporium,

@apophisfashion,

@apophisscardshop

Twitter: @apophisenterpr1, Tiktok:@apophisenterprise

Youtube: @sg1fan23477

Podcast: Apophis Chat Zone: https://open.spotify.com/show/5zXbrCLEV2xzCp8ybrfHsk?si=fb4d4fdbdce44dec

Newsletter: https://apophiss-newsletter-27c897.beehiiv.com/

I will be publishing more books, please keep an eye out for them. I love books, books are perfect for all.